The Wit
of the Scots

This book of Scottish wit and wisdom is dedicated to the many millions who still don't know what a Scotsman wears underneath his kilt!

The Wit
of the Scots

Compiled by

Gordon Irving

LESLIE FREWIN : LONDON

© Gordon Irving and Leslie Frewin Publishers Limited, 1969

First published 1969 by
Leslie Frewin Publishers Limited
15 Hay's Mews, Berkeley Square, London W1

This book has been set in Bembo,
printed by Anchor Press
and bound by William Brendon,
both of Tiptree, Essex

World Rights Reserved
09 096210 9

CONTENTS

Foreword

by Jimmy Logan

As a Scottish entertainer I can't help having some experience of the wit and humour of the nation to which I belong. Travels over the years to appear before audiences from Glasgow and Edinburgh to Vancouver and Los Angeles, from the London Palladium to New York's Carnegie Hall, have taken me in front of audiences of many kinds, and the pawky, gentle, yet often quite sophisticated wit of the Scots has helped me to communicate with so many.

Despite our frequent use of dialect, at first sight maybe a wee bit baffling to people outside Scotland, the humour of the Scots is appreciated – and understood. An American in Oklahoma or Oregon can understand it every bit as clearly as a Scots-descended Canadian in, say, Newfoundland or a Cockney lady in London.

Because of my profession, the telling of stories and the recounting of the best Scottish witticisms has been a special study of mine. I view the subject-matter from both sides of the footlights.

There is nothing more satisfying, I think, than telling a basic piece of wit four thousand miles away from your home town or country, and finding that a man or woman who has never been to your country – and who doesn't know you from Adam – can get the point of the joke or witticism, and laugh, either quietly or heartily.

To say that wit and humour are international is something of a cliché, of course, but then clichés are rarely off the beam.

Not so long ago it was discovered that Scottish and Bulgarian humour have something in common. It was revealed that a town called Gabrovo, in Bulgaria, specialises in the same kind of 'mean' and 'canny' jokes and witticisms as does the city of Aberdeen, in Scotland. The link is so strong that the press attaché in the Bulgarian Embassy in London wrote to the Scots seeking Aberdeen joke books for despatch to Bulgaria.

(Now, here is one further book of Scottish wit that can be added to his mailing list.)

The piece of Scottish wit I like best, I think, is as follows:

The pride of the Scot in his heritage and ancestry is an important part of his character. The scene is a loch in the Highlands, deserted, except for two stocky Highlanders fishing for brown trout, surely the sport of kings, in a country where the poacher is looked upon as a gentleman entitled to fish in any loch.

One Highlander is a MacLeod, the other a MacPherson and they are discussing their respective clans.

MACLEOD   You know, Macpherson, there was even a MacLeod fought beside Joan of Arc and was with her when she entered Orleans.

MACPHERSON   Ach, that's nothing, it was a MacPherson who assisted Bonnie Prince Charlie escape after the Battle of Culloden.

MACLEOD   Now, that's interesting because one of my ancestors was a General with the great Czar of Russia in 1610.

MACPHERSON	Ah, it was a MacPherson who fought the Viking raids in the North Coast of Scotland many years before that.
MACLEOD	There was a MacLeod with Boadicea when she fought to turn back the Roman legions.
MACPHERSON	That is nothing, one of my ancestors was with Noah in the Ark and he didn't see a MacLeod there.
MACLEOD	Of course not, did you ever hear of a Macleod who didn't have a boat of his own?

There is also a story of a Ferguson who found himself in London with only 6d left in his sporran. He was starving and could see that a fine fish supper could be his but it would cost 9d, so he pawned the 6d for 5d and sold the pawn ticket to an Irishman for 4d.

Most of Scotland's humour stems from our social conditions of the past. And from our history.

We have a hard, stern background, with many conflicts and problems. There have been many battles for the Scots – even against my friends the English!

That is why wit and humour, both on the stage and off, is, in many instances, built round repartee with Englishmen. The Scot may have been the underdog for years, but he likes to joke back, score against the stronger one, and smile as he registers a point in words.

Humour that tilts at the Irish and the Americans is also very much part of our tradition.

The story I like best in this most entertaining book is one Sir Harry Lauder used to tell about an elderly Scottish lady who sat in the front row at one of his shows (how well I personally know the type even today!) and listened all through his act without a trace of a smile. As she wended her way out of the hall, she looked at her friend, smiled, and whispered: 'Aye, aye. A grand wee comedian, yon man Lauder. But oh my, whit an awfy job A had tae keep frae laughin'!'

I think that about sums up the Wit of the Scots. We are a nation not given to over-enthusiasm or extrovert displays or wild, chuckling laughter. Too often a great English or American comedian has 'died standing up' on a Monday night at a Glasgow music-hall; the old Empire in Sauchie-hall Street was once dubbed 'the graveyard of the English comics'.

No, we like our wit and humour to be warm, gentle, wholesome and sincere, and Scots enjoy it often without that tell-tale smile. But we still have a wonderful heritage of humour and wit, as this book shows so clearly. It is a tradition to be cherished in an ever-changing world.

As you 'wachle' happily through *The Wit of the Scots*, I guarantee you'll have an 'awfy job tae keep frae laughin'.'

JL

Introduction

Among other good qualities, the Scots have been distinguished for humour – not for venomous wit, but for kindly, genial humour, which half loves what it laughs at – and this alone shows clearly enough that those to whom it belongs have not looked too exclusively on the gloomy side of the world.

James Anthony Froude, in Rectorial address at Edinburgh University

It requires a surgical operation to get a joke well into a Scotch understanding. Their only idea of wit, which prevails occasionally in the north and ... is so infinitely distressing to people of good taste, is laughing immoderately at stated intervals.

Sydney Smith

IT WAS STEPHEN LEACOCK who said that the two most distinctive humours are American and Scots. To anyone from north of Hadrian's Wall that is surely an unaccustomed and little-publicised tribute, and one of which I feel we ought to make much more.

Distinctive though both these humours may be there is, nevertheless, a difference, and an important one. The Scots joke about death; the Americans don't. The Scots crack jokes and witticisms about their own alleged meanness; the Americans, Jack Benny excepted, don't.

In subject-matter the two nations are the proverbial poles apart so far as categorising their humour targets is concerned.

The Americans – and a score of other nations, too – don't find nearly so much humour and wit in their church ministers, their cemeteries, their dollar reservoirs, or even on their death-beds and tombstones!

There is a sad, quiet and mournful streak about the Wit of the Scots. Much of it is expressed in the face of death, or in the auld grey churchyard on the hill, or in the deep moroseness of over-indulgence in more than a wee dram of good Scotch whisky.

If you analyse it by settings, then I'm afraid we Scots do, after all, take our humour rather seriously. But we are, I must emphasise, much more lightsome in outlook than Sydney Smith's description when he called us 'that land of Calvin, oat cakes and sulphur'.

I don't, of course, subscribe to the theory that every Scot is a born wit or humorist. Every nation has its varying degrees of humorists. Scotland, like many other lands, has probably more non-humorists than wits. But the latter make up for any dearth of seeing the lighter side of living by the quality and native richness of their wit.

Many of Scotland's best-known writers have championed the cause of wit. Wasn't it Sir Walter Scott, in fact, who said that 'life without mirth is like a lamp without oil'?

One important point must not be overlooked. The Scot – agree or disagree, as you wish – is very much what I choose to call a secret humorist. He quietly creates his wit and jokes as if they were an unpermitted diversion, frowned on by the authorities.

What has contributed to this? I think, possibly, it is the essential dullness of our Scottish towns and cities in the past, and the lack of that easy gaiety and lightness that pervades so much of English (especially rural) life. Another factor is the quite unnecessary dreariness and sternness that has dominated the Church and educational spheres of Scottish life over the years.

In contrast to this restraint, this feeling that it is a sin to be witty (which accounts for the pawky gentleness of much of Scots humour), a goodly proportion of our wit and fun is rough and coarse and outspoken, a probable reflection of an over-disciplined race rebelling against unnecessary seriousness.

Then there is the 'meanness' humour. This ubiquitous joke is, of course, not founded on fact. As I point out in my biography of Sir Harry Lauder, *Great Scot!*, it is a completely false image that has gone all round the world (and will go on doing so) simply because people love to laugh at ultra-canniness, and to poke fun at the skinflints among us. It is part of the 'insult' humour so beloved of sophisticates in many countries.

Much of the Wit of the Scots has been kept alive in the music-halls of Glasgow, Edinburgh and other centres. Although many feel they are a dying race, the kilted comedians cracking jokes against themselves and their kind have nurtured much of the pawky, gentle wit of their homeland, and it is intriguing to see how this type of humour is appreciated even more among the Scots exiles in Canada, the USA, Australia and New Zealand, grasping in modern lands far from the hills of home for a little bit of their native tradition.

The Scottish Church, while a very serious and often castigated establishment, has never failed, also, to laugh at itself beneath that austere façade so often presented to the world, and the Scots minister, in village, town and city, is the originator of many a happy item of wit and wisdom, as I trust this book will show. This is a welcome factor; the Church can smile when it likes.

I have devoted a special section to 'The Worthies'. These are the characters of a nation, the individualistic types, usually elderly, who have crystallised the sense of humour of their country in witticisms, anecdotes and sayings that surely stand the test of changing times.

The rich and often picturesque Scots dialect and vernacular, and much of the auld Scots tongue, lends a special flavour to a lot of our wit. It may, at times, bamboozle the Englishman or the foreigner by its quaintness, but many a gem of Scots wit and humour gains a distinctive national quality through its use.

While we may not always be intelligible to others, at least we are retaining the natural speech that comes from a spontaneous burst of humour.

The self-analysis of the Scot is also evident in much of his style of telling a joke or making a comment on life. Many a Scot screws up his eyes as he gives out with an observation; the quizzical look seems to suggest that he is shrewdly assessing the listener's reaction to his humour. This is the serious approach to wit, the sign that reveals a desire to achieve quality and results the next time around.

Then there is our Scotch whisky! Ah, happy thought! As

a nation we are renowned for the whisky we send all round the globe. But we also have a rather unfair image as whisky drinkers, imbibing overmuch of the native spirit, so they claim. Like the charges of ultra-thriftiness and meanness, this can also be a calumny.

If the Scots were not a people with a sense of humour they would surely not laugh at themselves when such items are put over to a critical world. The wit and humour of Scotsmen 'In Their Cups' is given a section to itself for this reason alone.

Finally, in tone with the dry wit of so many Scots on their death-beds, there is a special section which I have labelled 'In the Kirkyard'. Even on their tombstones Scots have and give the last laugh – in some very quotable epitaphs that reveal a sense of wit to the very end, and beyond it!

What can be wrong with a nation of men and women who, even six feet under the good earth, can wax so witty in humour against themselves?

Precious little, I say. By such standards they are surely the very Wit of the *Earth*!

G I

Meet the Scots

*Robert Burns, the poet, was attending church in Dumfries.
Sitting in the pew in front of him was a young lady, a Miss
Ainslie. The text of the sermon was a 'fierce denunciation of
obstinate sinners'. Burns, always with an eye to helping the
ladies, noticed the young girl frantically thumbing through the
pages of her Bible for the text. Scribbling a verse hurriedly, he
handed it to her. It read:*

> Fair Maid, you need not take the hint,
> Nor idle texts pursue;
> 'Twas guilty sinners that he meant,
> Not angels – such as you!

*   *   *

*Lord Elibank was told of Dr Samuel Johnson's definition of
oats – 'A grain which, in England, is generally given to horses,
but in Scotland supports the people'. To which he retorted:*

But where will you find such men – and such horses!

*   *   *

Lord Braxfield, distinguished Scots law lord, listened to an eloquent culprit at the bar, and told him:

Ye're a verra clever chiel, man, but ye wad be nane the waur o' a hanging.

*　　*　　*

John Buchan, author and politician:

An atheist is a man who has no invisible means of support.

*　　*　　*

Robert Louis Stevenson had this to say of the wedding institution:

Marriage is like life in this – that it is a field of battle, and not a bed of roses.

*　　*　　*

Andrew Carnegie, the Fife man who became a philanthropist and a wealthy steel magnate in America, in an analysis of the two sides of every Scotsman, the clinical and the sentimental, said:

Touch his head, and he will bargain and argue
　　with you to the last;
Touch his heart, and he falls upon your breast.

*　　*　　*

HE SAID HE WIS WAN
O' THE FLOWER PEOPLE
SO AH PLANTED HIM.

Mary Queen of Scots was being harangued by one of the English courtiers about the wisdom of Queen Elizabeth. She halted him in his eulogy and said:

Pray, sir, don't talk to me about the wisdom of a woman. I think I know my own sex pretty well, and can assure you that the wisest of us is only a little less a fool than the others.

* * *

Sir James M Barrie, author and playwright, once commented:

There are few more impressive sights in the world than a Scotsman on the make.

* * *

George Outram, the Glasgow poet, composed these lines on hearing a lady friend praising a certain reverend gentleman preacher's eyes:

> I cannot praise the Doctor's eyes,
>   I never saw his glance divine;
> He always shuts them when he prays,
>   And when he preaches he shuts mine.

* * *

Robert Burns went to a church service at Lamington, Lanarkshire, and found the place cold and uncomfortable, the weather chilly, and the sermon extremely poor. He left these lines on the pew:

As cauld a wind as ever blew,
A caulder kirk, and in't but few;
As cauld a preacher's ever spak'
Ye'll a' be het ere I come back.

*   *   *

On another occasion Robert Burns was holding forth in the King's Arms Inn in Dumfries and discussing the death of a fellow-townsman whose funeral was the following day. 'I wish you would lend me your black coat for the occasion,' said a friend. 'My own is in need of repair.' Burns replied that he would be attending the funeral himself and would therefore be unable to lend him his coat. Then he said:

I can recommend the most excellent substitute. Throw your character over your shoulders. That will be the blackest coat you ever wore in your lifetime.

*   *   *

Allan Ramsay, the poet, lived for a time in a remarkable house of octagonal shape on the Castle Hill of Edinburgh. He was very proud of the building, and regarded it as having exceptional beauty. Showing it one day to his friend Lord Elibank, the poet said his friends had told him it resembled a goose pie. To which Lord Elibank commented:

Indeed, Allan, now that I see you in it, I think the term is very properly applied.

*   *   *

Sir Harry Lauder was playing a theatre in Chicago when he invited an elderly lady on to the stage to dance with him in 'I Love A Lassie'. She agreed, but first informed him that she had driven thirty miles to see and hear him, only to get a seat on the stage. Lauder looked thoughtful for a moment, then replied:

But that's nothing, my dear lassie. I've just travelled five thousand miles to see you.

*　　*　　*

Sir Walter Scott, commenting on a common frailty of all who peruse the written word:

My friends arena' great book readers, but they are maistly a' grand book keepers.

*　　*　　*

An Englishman, after listening to a Scotsman deriding his race, protested that he was born an Englishman and hoped to die an Englishman. To which the Scot replied:

Man, man, hiv ye nae ambeetion?

*　　*　　*

Donald McGill, the comic-postcard 'king', concocted some favourite three-part joke lines in his drawings. One of his best known runs:

When you're born, they throw water over you.
When you're married, they throw rice over you,
And when you're dead, they throw dirt over you.

*   *   *

Another McGill witticism shows a buxom matron saying to a steward on a holiday boat:

Lunch? Just throw it overboard. It's quicker.

*   *   *

R B Cunninghame Graham, the writer:

Success, which touches nothing that it does not vulgarise, should be its own reward. In fact, rewards of any kind are but vulgarities.

*   *   *

Sean Connery, the 'James Bond' of the film world, who is an Edinburgh Scot, scoffs at the idea that Scots don't make dynamic lovers:

People imagine we Scots are all red-haired and about five feet small. It's fantastic. I reckon there is no race more romantic than the Scots.

*   *   *

Sir James Barrie told of this incident from his schooldays at Dumfries Academy:

Once a learned professor came to school to examine us. After several days of it, I decided to absent myself from the final proceedings. Other boys were sent in pursuit, and there was a hot chase until I discovered that, if I went slowly, they also went slowly; that, in short, they were as little desirous of returning to Lochaber as I was. . . .

I remember going to the station, and from a safe place watching the professor go off in his train, before I returned to the school to find, alas, that the exams were over. But my teacher had me that day; he told me the professor had wanted me back only to commend me for a confiscated book of sketches!

*　　　*　　　*

Lord Braxfield listened quietly to his butler as he complained of Lady Braxfield's manner to the servants. Then, equally quietly, he said:

Ye've gey little to complain o', man. Ye should be thankful ye're no' married tae her!

*　　　*　　　*

An anonymous philosopher – and a good guess is that he was a Scotsman – made this observation:

The human race is divided into two sections: first, Scotsmen; second, those who would like to be Scotsmen.

*   *   *

Andrew Carnegie, on a visit home from America to his native Scotland, was looking for a piece of land in the Highlands, but stipulated it must have an echo. Sandy had a few acres to sell and, knowing of Carnegie's wish, got together with his friend Donald about the echo. They agreed that Donald would go up the hill and answer in like manner to the spoken words below. Carnegie was impressed with the property, and immediately tested it for the echo. He called out 'Hello', and the word came back clearly: 'Hello'. Several other words were tried. Then Carnegie crossed Sandy up and cried out: 'I've got a bottle o' whisky.' Whereupon the echo came back, loud and clear:

I'll be doon in a minute!

*   *   *

Robert Burns expresses all the wit and humanity of honest men in his famous Selkirk Grace, first said at the table of the Earl of Selkirk, and quoted at banquets and dinners all over the world:

> Some hae meat and canna eat,
> And some wad eat that want it,
> But we hae meat, and we can eat,
> And sae the Lord be thanket.

*   *   *

Sir Walter Scott was attending the funeral service of the Earl of Buchan, an eccentric nobleman. The body ought to have been carried into the chapel, where it was to be interred, feet first. Instead, the head of the coffin was first in, and one mourner remarked: 'We have brought the Earl's head in the wrong way.' To which Scott retorted:

Never mind, my friends. His Lordship's head was turned when he was alive. It is not worth our while to shift it now.

* * *

Thomas Carlyle, the philosopher:

Great men taken up in any way are profitable friends. The history of the world is but the biography of great men.

* * *

The late Finlay Currie, veteran actor of films and television, was asked, at ninety, if he would like to live to be a hundred, and smiled:

Not really, though I do come from a long-lived family. My grandfather reached a hundred, and then he was shot – by a jealous husband.

* * *

Robert Burns was standing on the quay at Greenock when a rich merchant from the town suddenly fell into the harbour. A sailor dived in and rescued him. The merchant put his hand in his pocket and gave the sailor a shilling. When the watching crowd protested at the smallness of the sum, Burns told them to stop the protests, and added:

This gentleman is the best judge of the value of his own life.

*   *   *

Sir Compton Mackenzie, indefatigable writer, speaker, broadcaster and conversationalist, diagnosed his own main fault thus:

The trouble with me is that I love to talk, and I love people. Indeed, I've got to take a holiday now and then to get away from them.

*   *   *

Sir Compton had the knack, in a long career, of being able to laugh at himself. He once quipped:

As one of the few men still alive who was commissioned by Queen Victoria, I often wonder whether I should not be stuffed and stuck with the other relics in the Imperial War Museum.

*   *   *

William McGonagall, the inept 'poet' from Dundee, claimed Edinburgh as his birthplace, and wrote these lines about the rival city of Glasgow:

'Tis beautiful to see the ships passing to and fro,
Laden with goods for the high and the low;
So let the beautiful city of Glasgow flourish,
And may the inhabitants always find food
    their bodies to nourish.

*   *   *

Sir Harry Lauder and Robert Burns both had the very human quality of knowing how difficult it is, sometimes, to get out of bed and start work. Burns said:

Up in the mornin's no' for me,
Up in the morning early.

To which Sir Harry Lauder replied in song:

Oh, it's nice to get up in the mornin',
But it's nicer to lie in your bed.

*   *   *

Donald McGill, appearing on 'What's My Line?' on television, was asked by the late Gilbert Harding: 'So you do these dirty postcards?' He replied:

No, that is incorrect. I am a Seaside Artist.

*   *   *

Sir James M Barrie:

It is not true that woman was made from man's rib. She was really made from his funny bone.

Every man who is high up loves to think that he has done it all himself; and the wife smiles, and lets it go at that.

Them that has china plates themsel' is the maist careful not to break the china plates of others.

We are all of us failures – at least, the best of us are.

I am not young enough to know everything.

*　　*　　*

William McGonagall, in a tribute to 'The Beautiful City of Glasgow':

> Then there is a grand picture gallery,
> Which keepers thereof are paid a very large salary;
> Therefore, citizens of Glasgow, do not fret or worry,
> For there is nothing like it in Edinburry.

*　　*　　*

The Hon Henry Erskine, in an Edinburgh of yesteryear, declined the loan of a silk gown from a retiring Lord Advocate on being appointed to that high office:

Never shall it be said that Henry Erskine adopted the *abandoned habits* of his predecessor.

* * *

James Boswell, biographer of Samuel Johnson, hit out thus at a friend who was unable to indulge in the kind of Scots raillery known as 'roasting':

Sir, you're an exceedingly good-natured man, to be sure; but I can give you a better reason for your never roasting any. Sir, you never roast because you have got no fire.

* * *

King James the Fifth of Scotland, on his death-bed, on being informed of the birth of a daughter:

God's will be done. It cam' wi' a lass, and it'll gang wi' a lass.

* * *

Robert Louis Stevenson:

Marriage is one long conversation, chequered by disputes.

If they only married when they fell in love, most people would die unwed.

Give me the young man who has brains enough to make a fool of himself.

If a man is lucky enough to be born a Scot, he must pay for the privilege, like any other advantage.

In marriage a man becomes slack and selfish, and undergoes a fatty degeneration of his moral being.

Wealth is only useful for two things: a yacht and a string quartette.

Failure is the only high-road to success.

There must be something wrong in me, or I would not be popular.

To marry is to domesticate the Recording Angel. Once you are married, there is nothing left for you, not even suicide, but to be good.

He sows hurry and reaps indigestion.

It is better to be a fool than to be dead.

Youth is wholly experimental.

In the Kirkyard

This epitaph was found in a churchyard in Dumfriesshire, in the South of Scotland:

> Here lies Andrew McPherson,
> Who was a peculiar person;
> He stood six feet two
> Without his shoe,
> And was slew
> At Waterloo.

*   *   *

Verse in the wall of Elgin Cathedral:

> The world is a city full of streets,
> And death the mercat that all men meets,
> If lyfe were a thing that monie could buy,
> The poor could not live, and the rich would not
>   die.

*   *   *

'HE SAYS IT'S BAD ENOUGH WORRYIN'
ABOOT PRICES WITHOUT HUVIN' AN
INCOME TAE WORRY ABOOT AS WEEL!'

Epitaph in an East Coast churchyard:

> JPP
> Provost of Dundee,
> Hallelujah,
> Hallelujee.

* * *

Without comment – obviously from a Scot who did not hate himself:

> Here lies the laird o' Lundie,
> Sic transit gloria mundi.

* * *

Epitaph dictated by one John So, of Inverkip, and self-composed:

> Here lies John So,
> So so did he so,
> So did he live,
> So did he die,
> So so did he so,
> So let him lie.

* * *

There is an obvious tilt at the argumentative talent of woman in these lines, found in a Forfar cemetery:

'Tis here that Tibby Allan lies,
  'Tis here, or here aboot,
But no one till the Resurrection day,
  Shall the very spot dispute.

*   *   *

Epitaphs in a churchyard at Hoddam, Dumfriesshire:

Here lyes a man, who all his mortal life,
  Past mending clocks, but could not mend his wife,
The 'larum of his bell was ne'er sae shrill
  As was her tongue – aye clacking like a mill.
But now he's gane – oh! whither nane can tell –
  I hope beyond the sound o' Mally's bell.

*   *   *

Here lie the bones o' Tammy Messer,
  Of Tarry woo' he was a dresser;
He had some fau'ts and mony merits,
  And died o' drinking ardent spirits.

*   *   *

Found on an old tombstone on the island of Skye:

Here lie the bones
O' Tonald Jones,
The wale o' men
For eating scones.

Eating scones
And drinking yill,
Till his last moans
He took his fill.

*   *   *

A strolling Scots musician named Abercromby wrote this epitaph
for his tombstone in a Highland churchyard:

Here Crummy lies enclosed in wood
　　Full six feet one and better
When tyrant death grim o'er him stood
　　He faced him like a hatter.
Now lies he low without a boot
　　Free from a world of bustle,
And silent now is Crummy's flute
　　And awful dry his whistle.

*   *   *

This verse has been found in various churchyards in Scotland:

Our life is but a winter day,
　　Some only breakfast and away,
Others to dinner stay and are full fed,
　　The oldest man but sups and goes to bed,
Large is his debt that lingers out the day,
　　He that goes soonest has the least to pay.

*   *   *

Epitaph in a Scottish churchyard:

> Here lies interr'd a man o' micht.
>> They ca'd him Malcolm Downie;
> He lost his life ae market nicht,
>> By fa'ing aff his pownie.

Aged 37 years.

*   *   *

'THE WEE SOWL IS MORE INCLINED TAE COME OOT O' THE LOCH NOW THAT THE SCOTTISH NATIONALISTS ARE GETTIN' THE UPPER HAND'

From a kirkyard in Haddington, East Lothian:

> Hout, Atropos, hard-hearted Hag,
> To cut the sheugh of Jamie Craig;
> For had he lived a wheen mae years,
> He had been owre tough for all your shears.

*   *   *

This one was spotted on a gravestone in the North of Scotland:

> Dry up your tears and weep no more,
> I am not dead but gone before,
> Remember me and bear in mind,
> You have not long to stay behind.

*   *   *

Epitaph in a country graveyard on the shores of the Firth of Forth:

> In this churchyard lies Eppie Coutts,
> Either here or hereaboots;
> But whaur she is there's nane can tell,
> Till Eppie rise and tell hersel'.

*   *   *

On a gravestone in Peterhead:

> Wha lies here?
> John Sim, ye needna' spier.

Hullo, John, is that you?
Aye, aye, but I'm deid noo.

*   *   *

An epitaph from Fife:

Here lies my good and gracious Auntie,
   Whom Death has packed in his portmanty,
Threescore and ten years God did gift her
   And here she lies, wha de'il daurs lift her?

*   *   *

*This verse comes from a tombstone in Annandale, in the South
of Scotland (note that 'wame'=belly):*

I, Jacky Bell, o' Brakenbrow, lyes under this stane,
   Five of my awn sons laid it on my wame;
I liv'd aw my deyes, but sturt or strife
   Was man o' my meat, and master o' my wife;
If you've done better in your time than I did in mine,
   Tak' the stane aff my wame, and lay it on thine.

*   *   *

*A Scot who built a wall round the churchyard of Desken, near
Cullen, Banffshire, had these lines engraved on his tombstone:*

Hic jacet Joannes Anderson, Aberdoniensis,
Who built this churchyard dyke at his own expenses.

*   *   *

This epitaph is a near-classic from a Scottish graveyard:

> Here lies I, Martin Elginbrodde:
>> Hae mercy o' my soul, Lord God,
> As I wad do, were I Lord God,
>> And ye were Martin Elginbrodde.

*   *   *

Epitaph found in an old kirkyard in the Scottish Border country:

> Here lies the Horner of Horncliffe,
>> Puir Tam Gordon, cauld and stiff,
> Wha in this narrow hole was puttin'
>> For his lawless love of wedder mutton.

*   *   *

Obviously, Scots of the past thought alike:

> Here lyes
> Duncan Smedholm
> farmer in Mount Progeny
> who was born 9th January 1751–2
> and dyed 11th October 1836
> aged 84
> who had 41 legitimate children
> by two wives

*   *   *

. . . and on a gravestone in Aberdeenshire:

Erected to the Memory of Alexander Gray, some time farmer in Mill of Burns, who died in the 96th year of his age, having had thirty-two legitimate children by two wives.

At the Music-Hall

The late Tommy Morgan, gravel-voiced jester of the old Glasgow music-hall, was lunching in an uppity Belfast hotel. Waiters fussed all around. The best in wine and food was offered to him, a popular figure, for he was starring in a city theatre. An elegant and rather posh head-waiter approached and asked: 'Now, will you be havin' a bit of partridge, Mr Morgan?' To which the comedian replied:

A bit! Whit dae ye mean, a bit! Bring us a hale yin each!

* * *

Scots music-hall comedians are jesters off-stage as well as on. Alec Finlay, the kilted comedy star from Glasgow, had to use colleague-in-fun Jimmy Logan's theatre dressing-room for a Sunday-night concert. He tells:

I arrived to find that he had tied up all the drawers and wardrobes with thick rope, and had put giant-sized padlocks on all the cases. But I got revenge two nights later. I got his orchestra to play 'Happy Birthday' and sent him a dozen gift-boxes, each one packed with bits of his rope and padlocks.

* * *

Kenneth McKellar, the internationally known Scottish singer, was appearing in the same show as comedian Alec Finlay, renowned as a practical joker. In one number Kenneth sang a song while standing on a pair of steps, picking apples from a tree. One night Alec covered the apples in varnish, and, as Kenneth explained:

Every time I picked an apple, it stuck to the gloves I was wearing. I had to keep singing and smiling at the audience, yet all the time I was frantically trying to shake the apples into a basket I had. In the end I chucked both apples and gloves into the basket, and got on with the song. And there was wee Alec standing in the wings, 'killing' himself with laughter!

*   *   *

Lex McLean, the Glasgow music-hall comedian, has this favourite McLean-ism:

Laugh and the world laughs with you. Quarrel with the wife and you sleep alone.

*   *   *

About his career, McLean says:

In my early days the notion that I might become a comedian struck me. It would be easier, I thought, than . . . working!

*   *   *

Chic Murray, the Scot with the casual style of ridiculous patter:

I met a pal I hadn't seen for some time. He was sitting in the cabin of a truck, and he said: 'I'm a truck driver now.' Mebbe he was telling me in case I thought he had bought it for the occasion.

* * *

So I opened the door. Of course, I had to open it just to get out.

* * *

D'you know, it's amazing. I can look at a person and say whether I know him or not. It's a gift I seem to have.

* * *

Kenneth McKellar:

An African native wrote saying that if I sent him a dozen photographs of myself he would bless me. I sent him the pictures next day! I should hate ever to get on the wrong side of a witch-doctor.

* * *

The great Sir Harry Lauder, Scotland's famed minstrel, found it tough going on a concert-party tour early in his career. Visiting Stenhousemuir, in Central Scotland, he came on a poster for his

*show, which hadn't exactly been setting the heather on fire.
'This poster had got mixed up with another poster for a religious
service in the same hall,' said Sir Harry. The juxtaposition of
the placards resulted in this billing:*

Only Appearance of

HARRY
LAUDER

The Audience Will Join In
Singing The Hymn 'Thank God
From Whom All Blessings Flow'

*　　　*　　　*

*Entertainment stars may have to cavort, frolic and look silly on
the stage, but they have a purpose, a most important one. Sir
Harry Lauder explained it thus:*

Och, aye, laddie, it's a hard life. But mind ye, there's no'
much use in bein' daft if ye're no' tae be well peyed for it!

*　　　*　　　*

*Scottish music-hall comedians for years have loved to tell the
story of the American tourist who was keen to see the bonnie
banks o' Loch Lomond and the Trossachs. He hired an old Scots
guide, and as they rounded a bend in the road, the American
asked: 'What's that little pool over there?'*

*Said the Scot: 'Pool! Man, that's Loch Lomond, famous in
song and story.'*

45

'Well, then, we could do with that in Noo York,' said the American.

Sandy replied: 'Nae trouble at a'. Ye can get it ower fast enough.'

'How do you mean, my man?'

To which Sandy made the now-classic retort:

Weel, a' ye need is a few miles o' pipe, an' if ye can sook as well as ye can blaw, it will be ower the Atlantic in nae time.

* * *

Sir Harry Lauder told of an old Scots lady who sat in the front row at one of his shows, and listened to his entire comedy act without a trace of a smile. Later, she told a friend:

Aye, aye! Yon's a grand wee comedian, Harry Lauder. A had an awfy job tae keep frae laughin'.

* * *

For many years a favourite music-hall phrase of the Scots comedian has been the 'Glesca-ised' (Glasgow) version of a conductor's admonition to a passenger. It means, in polite English, 'Would you kindly descend from the bus?' In the colloquial Glasgow speech it is put over as:

Cum-oan – Getaff !

* * *

'AND I SPEAK TO YOU AS A TRUE SCOT!'

Sir Harry Lauder was thinking aloud one day as he chatted with his friend, A C Astor, the theatrical ventriloquist, when the latter said that he might some day write a book about 'The Lauder I Know'. Quick as a flash, Harry retorted, with a grin:

Be careful, Arthur, or I'll come back and haunt ye.

*   *   *

Stanley Baxter, the stage and television comedy actor, who went to school in Glasgow, found that a touch of wit worked wonders in the classroom:

Whenever a teacher showed signs of getting angry, I tried to make her laugh. If I succeeded, I didn't get the belt.

*   *   *

Stanley Baxter has a flair for conjuring up the telling phrase that wittily sums up all the gusty flavour of the Glasgow vernacular. He tells of the typical wee Glasgow chap who saunters across the floor in a city dance-hall, and asks a fair damsel to dance. Simply, but in most picturesque Glasgow, he says:

URYEFURUP? ('Are you for up?')

*   *   *

Here are some more of the Baxter gems of local wit (with the very necessary translation for 'foreigners'):

Atzajinkies (Isn't it exquisite!)

48

Drapdeid (Please do not annoy me!)

Seezdoonajeelipeece (I'm hungry and require some sustenance)

Fella fellaffacaur (A man has fallen off a vehicle and is involved in a road accident)

The Worthies

The Reverend Robert Shirra, of Kirkcaldy, Fife, was reading from the 116th Psalm, 'I said in my haste, all men are liars.' Breaking off, he added the quiet side-remark:

Aye, Dauvid, an' if ye had lived in *this* parish, ye might hae said it at your *leisure*.

*　　*　　*

An American tourist drove his Cadillac into a tiny and deserted Scottish village, and asked a native: 'Say, what do you do in this God-forsaken spot when it rains?' The old worthy replied, quietly:

Weel, sir, we just dinna interfere.

*　　*　　*

The old gravedigger at Sorn, in Ayrshire, was asked how business was. He replied:

Oh, very poorly . . . very poorly indeed. I havena' buried a livin' soul for six weeks.

*　　*　　*

King Edward the Seventh, when Prince of Wales, was touring the West of Scotland with the Duke of Argyll. On one of their walks they were overtaken by a country postman, who stopped his horse and asked the travellers if they would care for a lift. The Duke took the back seat of the gig, and the Prince the front, beside the postman. After five minutes, the postman asked the Prince: 'Wha's that sittin' behind ye?' Said the Prince: 'The Duke of Argyll.'

Postman: 'Oh, aye.' (Silence for a few moments, then. . .) 'And wha are you?'

Prince: 'I'm the Prince of Wales.'

Postman: 'Oh, aye. I'm beginnin' tae see. Ye'll be wonderin' wha I am.'

Prince: 'Yes, I should like to know.'

Whereupon the postman leant over confidentially towards the Prince, and whispered:

Dinna tell anybody, but I'm the Shah o' Persia!

*   *   *

At one time the population of Lockerbie, Dumfriesshire, was largely composed of Johnstones and Jardines. A poor benighted traveller, on pleading in vain for assistance, was driven to exclaim: 'Are there no Christians here?' He received the reply:

No, we're a' Johnstones and Jardines!

*   *   *

A rather similar story concerns an Englishman who was travelling through the Highlands and came to an inn near a village. Seeing nobody around, he knocked on the door, but received no reply. So he opened the door and walked in. He spied a man lying on a bed and asked him: 'Are there no Christians in this house?' Whereupon the man replied:

No, sir, none. We are all Camerons.

* * *

The Rev Mr Scott, of the Cowgate in Edinburgh, didn't see eye to eye with his congregation. Preaching one Sunday on Job, he said:

My brethren, Job, in the first place, was a sairly tried man. Job, in the second place, was an uncommonly patient man. Job, in the third place, never preached here in the Cowgate. Fourthly, and lastly, if Job had preached here, God help his patience.

* * *

The minister called on a laird in Fife to ask for a donation to a fund for putting a stove into the cold church. The laird expostulated:

Cauld, sir, cauld! Then warm them up wi' your doctrine, sir. John Knox never askit for a stove in *his* kirk.

* * *

Kirkpatrick Macmillan, a country blacksmith from Courthill, in Dumfriesshire, in the South of Scotland, devised the world's first pedal-driven bicycle, and rode on it seventy miles over bumpy roads to Glasgow in June, 1842. All along his route he was taken for 'The Devil on Wheels'. Of his arrival in the Gorbals, on the south side of Glasgow, he said afterwards:

I had the bad luck tae knock ower a wee girlie. They hauled me afore the magistrate, an' he fined me five shillin's – for speedin' at eight miles an hour. But he liked my invention so much that he peyed the five shillin's himsel'.

*   *   *

A Scots newspaper reporter, commenting on the Macmillan arrival in the 'Glasgow Courant' of June, 1842, wrote:

This invention, we are confident, will not supersede the railway.

*   *   *

'Did ye ken,' asked Donald, 'that Sandy MacNab was ta'en up for stealin' a coo?' Replied Donald:

Hoot, toot, the stupit bodie! Could he no' hae bocht it, an' no peyed for it?

*   *   *

Lord Eskgrove, a Scottish judge, sentencing a tailor for murdering a soldier, told the accused man:

And not only did you murder him, whereby he was bereaved of his life, but you did thrust, or push, or pierce, or project, or propel the lethal weapon through the belly-band of his regimental breeches, which were His Majesty's.

*   *   *

Hislop, in his 'Book of Scottish Anecdotes', tells of a certain elderly Scotsman named Pittoddles:

When his third wife de'ed, he got married upon the Laird o' Blaithershin's aughteenth daughter, that wis sister to Jemina, that wis married until Tam Flumexer, that wis first and second cousin to the Pottoddleses, whase brither became laird afterwards, and married Blaithershin's Baubie – and that way Jemima became, in a kind o' way, her ain niece and her ain aunty.

*   *   *

Willie Hamilton, not over-endowed with worldly intelligence, and known as the 'daft man' of his district, was wasting time by the side of a loch near Ayr. Three young girls came along and started discussing whether they should venture on the ice. One of the girls suggested that Willie should be asked to walk on it first. To which he replied:

Och, A'm mebbe a wee bit daft, but A'm no' ill-bred. After you, ma ladies!

*   *   *

Rev Dr Norman MacLeod, walking down the fashionable Buchanan Street in Glasgow, with a business-man friend, was saluted by a bishop and then by the latter's valet. He was asked: 'Who was that man with the collar on?' To which he replied:

Oh, you mean the man who saluted just now. That was the *valet* of the shadow of death.

*　　*　　*

A wise old Scotsman, asked to give the meaning of the word 'metaphysics,' said:

Weel, it's like this. When the pairty that listens disna ken what the pairty that speak means, an' when the pairty that speaks disna ken what he means himsel', that's metapheesics.

*　　*　　*

Definition of love, by a Scots village character:

A yeukieness o' the heart that the hand canna claw.

*　　*　　*

Mr Thom, a noted preacher, of Govan, was delivering a sermon before the magistrate one Sunday when he suddenly halted and said:

Dinna snore sae loud, Bailie Broon, ye'll wauken the Provost.

*　　*　　*

An old lady, commenting on the young minister's sermon, said it had only three faults:

First, it was read. Second, it wasna' weel read. And thirdly, it wasna worth readin'.

*   *   *

An elderly Scotswoman was asked, on her way home from church, how the minister had fared with his sermon that morning. She replied:

How did he get on? Och, he just stood an' threw stanes at us, an' never missed wi' ane o' them. My certie, but yon was preaching!

*   *   *

A worthy minister from Edinburgh, a noted preacher, was entering Drury Lane Theatre, London, for a pantomime performance when a hand tapped him on the shoulder, and a man from his home city said: 'Oh, Dr McGregor, whit wad the folk at hame say if I tell't them I saw you here?' The minister replied:

Indeed, they widna believe you, so you needna bother to tell them.

*   *   *

A Scots dominie (schoolmaster) asked a new pupil how many brothers he had. The youngster replied:

Twa leevin' an' ane mairret! (Two living and one married)

*　　*　　*

An old ploughman saw a crowd collecting at a Highland railway station, all keen to catch a glimpse of the Prince of Wales as he passed by in the Royal train. Pushing his way through the mob, he asked what was happening. On being told, he replied:

Michty me! If I had kent that, I wadna hae run here sae fast. I thocht it wis a fight.

*　　*　　*

The picturesqueness and power of the Scottish language is reflected in the comment of Rev Thomas Mitchell, minister of Lamington, who, in praying for suitable harvest weather, expressed himself:

O Lord, gie us nane o' your rantin', tantin', tearin' winds, but a thunnerin', dunnerin', dryin' wind.

Laughing at Death

Auld Sandy was giving instructions for his own funeral. He told his son:

Aye, Jock, ye'll just gang roon the entire company an' see that they ha'e a wee dram. Syne, ye'll gang roon an' see that they ha'e anither (pause). An', seein' as I'll no' be there masel, I'll just ha'e mine the noo!

*   *   *

(note 'fash' = worry)
Another Scot was dying. 'Aye!' said his wife, as she sat tearfully by his bedside, 'for fifty years you've brought me up a cup o' tea tae ma bed in the mornin'. You've been richt guid, Sandy. Whit'll A dae when you're no' here tae get me it?' To which Sandy, in his dying breath, retorted:

Och, dinna fash yoursel', wumman! You can aye buy yoursel' a wee gas ring.

*   *   *

A minister was consoling a dying Highlander when suddenly the old man asked him: 'Is there ony whisky in Heaven?' Noting the minister's surprised look, he added the explanation:

Ye ken, meenister, it's no' that I care for it, but it looks awfy weel on the table.

*   *   *

The old Scots lady lay dying. She looked up and asked her husband if he would do her just one small favour before she went. 'John,' she asked, 'on the day o' the funeral I'd like ye tae ride in the same coach as ma mother.' To which John replied:

A' richt, Janet. I'll dae that tae please ye. But ye've completely spoilt the day for me.

*   *   *

Another elderly Scots lady lay dying in the middle of a terrible thunderstorm in the Highlands. She started to speak, and the relatives leaned nearer to hang on to her whispered words. Ever so faintly she was heard to say:

Ech, sirs, whit a nicht for me to be fleein' through the air!

*   *   *

An old Scots beadle or church-officer was opening up a grave before a funeral when he took a violent attack of coughing. The minister remarked: 'That's a very bad cough you've got, Jock.' To which the beadle replied:

Aye, it's no' very gude, you're richt. But there's a hantle fouk lyin' aboot here that wud be gey glad o't.

*   *   *

The old man was dying and fast slipping away. His wife bent over his bedside and asked (note 'baps' = scones):

Wullie, Wullie, as lang's ye can speak, are ye for your funeral baps roond – or square?

* * *

A minister was officiating on the occasion of a funeral. As he was about to return thanks after the service of wine and cake, the beadle or church-officer whispered in his ear:

Be as dreich (lengthy) as ye can, sir, for the glasses are frae Glasgow, an' I hae to wash them a' afore we lift the corpse.

* * *

Lord Hume, who believed in being self-sufficient, commented:

I ha'e come to the conclusion, lang syne, that when a man puts his property into the hands o' a lawyer, his body into the hands o' a doctor, and his soul into the hands o' a minister, he micht just as well lie doon in his kailyard and dee.

* * *

A not-so-subtle story concerns the coffin that popped out of a hearse as it was being driven up a hill to a cemetery in Maryhill, Glasgow. It slid back down the hill and across the street into a

chemist's shop. As it was crossing the floor, the man inside sat up and asked the chemist:

Say, sirr, hiv ye gote onythin' tae stoap ma coffin?

*   *   *

It was a merry gathering in the eighteenth century. One neighbour thought the laird looked rather strange. 'Whit gars Garscadden luik sae gash?' he asked the man next to him. The latter replied:

Och, Garscadden's been wi' his Maker these twa oors. I saw him step awa' but I didna like to disturb the good company.

*   *   *

Auld Sandy felt that the end was near. 'Aye, Jenny,' he told his wife, 'I'm thinking it canna be lang noo. I feel as if this very nicht the end wad come.' Jenny thought a moment, looked pensive, and said:

Indeed, Sandy, if it were the Lord's will, it wad be rale convenient, for the coo's gaun to calve, and I dinna weel see hoo I'm to be able to attend to you baith.

*   *   *

An Englishman visiting Scotland in the eighteenth century remarked:

A Scottish funeral is indeed merrier than an English holiday.

Aye Canny!

Are Scotsmen really mean with their money? Do they keep moths in their sporrans? Sir Harry Lauder propagated the image throughout the world, and millions keep it up in wisecrack and anecdote. True or false – and anyone who has visited Scotland or met the Scots will know the answer – it is nevertheless a theory that has created enough fodder for a million jokes and witticisms. The real laugh is, of course, that most of them are inspired by . . . Scots!

*   *   *

'Life' Magazine reported:

The first time a Scotchman used the free air at the garage, he blew out all four tyres!

*   *   *

A man from Paisley was describing the Niagara Falls to a friend:

Aye, it's naethin' but . . . a perfect waste o' water!

*   *   *

George Heriot, an Edinburgh jeweller and money-lender, of the seventeenth century, visited the Royal apartments at the Palace of Holyroodhouse, in Edinburgh, and found King James the Sixth basking before a fire of exotic perfumed wood from the Orient. 'Your Majesty, if you will step along to my shop, I will show you an even more costly flame,' said Heriot. The King made his way to Heriot's tiny shop and found an unspectacular fire in the grate. Then the jeweller took from his pocket an IOU note from the King for two thousand pounds, casually tossed it on to the fire, and asked:

Now, sire, is Your Majesty's fire or mine the more expensive one?

*　　*　　*

A Scot who preferred to stay anonymous gave this description of his fellow-countrymen:

A Scotsman is someone who keeps the Sabbath day – and every other darned thing he can lay his hands on.

*　　*　　*

A publican, faced with the rising price of whisky and diminished stock, was asked why he was charging a higher price for what seemed to be a smaller glass. He replied:

Well, you see, you might call this a measure of expediency.

*　　*　　*

Favourite witticism of the Scots:

'An Aberdeen street on a flag-day.'

*　　*　　*

An Aberdeen man on holiday in Palestine arrived at the Sea of Galilee and found, to his horror, that the hire of a pleasure-boat was 3s 6d an hour.

'Three and sixpence!' he exclaimed. 'We can get a boat in Aberdeen for sixpence.'

E

'Ah,' said the boatman, 'but this is Palestine. And these are the waters on which our Lord walked.'

To which the Aberdonian replied: 'Nae wonder He walked, then. Look what ye chairge for a boat.'

*   *   *

In one of Donald McGill's comic postcards the boots in a hotel is found cleaning the shoes outside a bedroom door. He says:

I can't clean them downstairs, sir; there's a Scotch gent inside and he won't let go of the laces.

*   *   *

In the Sir Walter Scott story 'Old Mortality', the Laird of Milnwood lies on his death-bed. As he reaches his final words, he turns to his old housekeeper, Alison Wilson, asks her to take away the wax candle burning at his bedside, and remarks:

A tallow candle's guid enough tae see tae dee wi'.

*   *   *

The traditional canniness of the Scot is reflected in this gem of conversational advice, offered by Robert Burns:

> But still keep something to yoursel'
> Ye scarcely tell to ony.

*   *   *

Carefulness and canniness in handing out praise is reflected in the story of a dear old lady of sixty-five who went up to Lex McLean, the Scottish comedian, after one of his theatre shows, and said:

Lex McLean, you're a terrible man . . . but, my, you're awfu' guid!

*   *   *

On a Saturday night in a Scottish village members of the Salvation Army were saying prayers and singing hymns. At the intermission a young Army lass went up to an elderly Scotsman and held out the familiar tambourine:

'Will you give a shilling to the Lord?' she asked.
   'Hoo auld are ye, ma lassie?'
   'I'm just sixteen.'
   To which the old man replied:
   'Weel, I'm seventy-nine, an' I'll be seein' Him before you, so I'll just hand it tae Him masel'.'

*   *   *

The eternal canniness of the Scot is shown in his brevity of words. A degree of dry wit and humour is in this conversation, overheard as a man inquired at a shop door about a tartan plaid hanging up for sale. (It should be explained that the word 'oo' means 'wool')
Customer: Oo?
Shopkeeper: Aye, oo.
Customer: A' oo? (All wool?)
Shopkeeper: Aye, a' oo.

Customer: A' a'e oo? (All one wool?)
Shopkeeper: Ou, aye, a' a'e oo.

* * *

The minister, calling for a good response to a special collection appeal, told the congregation that some of the parishioners were putting buttons in the plate instead of money. He ended his plea:

If ye're still determined tae put buttons on the plate, please bring your own buttons. Dinna clip them aff the cushions!

* * *

The stock and corny joke about a Scotsman concerns the man who went on holiday:

He took with him a clean shirt and a pound note. When he arrived back home, he hadn't changed either of them.

* * *

Policemen in Glasgow, in the mid-nineteenth century, used to call out the hours in the morning and, at the same time, proclaim the state of the weather. Householders heard them in the early hours, underneath their windows, calling phrases like 'Five o'clock – and a fine mornin',' or 'Five o'clock and a rainy mornin'.' One policeman, finding the climatic conditions almost indescribable, compromised by calling out:

Six o'clock – and a funny mornin'.

* * *

The Hon Henry Erskine was a guest at a justiciary dinner in Perth, presided over by Lord Kames. His lordship, with a reputation for being careful with his money, did not produce the usual quantity of claret. The conversation turned on Sir Charles Hardy's fleet, then being blockaded by the French. Upon which Erskine said:

They are, like us, confined to port.

*   *   *

Lex McLean, the Glasgow music-hall comedian, tells of the Aberdonian who absent-mindedly dropped a one-pound note into the collection plate in church. He couldn't sleep for thinking about it. So, whenever the plate came round again, he just nodded to the church elder, and shouted:

Season!

*   *   *

This newspaper placard is alleged to have been spotted in – where else! – Union Street, Aberdeen:

TWO TAXIS
COLLIDE

—

24 PASSENGERS
INJURED

Wise Cracks

The learned Dr Samuel Johnson, always ready with good humour to take a Scotsman down a peg or two, was delving into a large dish of haggis when a Scots lady asked him how he liked it. 'Very good for hogs, madam, I believe,' he replied. The Scots lady smiled ever so sweetly and replied:

Then please, let me help you to some more of it!

*　　*　　*

Lord Rockville, third son of the Earl of Aberdeen, a leading Scottish judge, was also noted for his fondness of the bottle. Arriving late one evening at his Edinburgh club, he announced with great solemnity:

Gentlemen, I have just met with the most extraordinary adventure that ever occurred to a human being. As I was walking along the Grassmarket all of a sudden the street rose up and struck me on the face.

*　　*　　*

The celebrated preacher Edward Irving (an ancestor of the compiler of this book, incidentally) had been lecturing in Dumfries and a local wit was asked by the Rev Walter Dunlop what he thought of him. The man replied: 'Och, the man's crackit!' (silly). Mr Dunlop smiled, patted the man on the shoulder, and said:

Ah, but never mind, Willie. Ye'll often see a bright light shinin' through a crack.

*   *   *

Lunardi ascended in a balloon from Edinburgh, and came down again near a clergyman's house in Fife, across the Firth of Forth. He told the clergyman: 'We have been at the gate of Heaven since we went up.' The clergyman replied:

Then it is a pity you didn't go in; you may never be so near again.

*   *   *

R B Cunninghame Graham, the writer, was asked by a lady if a rumour she had heard about his Royal lineage was true. He replied:

Madam, if I had my rights, I would be king. And what a six weeks that would be!

*   *   *

A minister told one of his congregation, in a North of Scotland town, that he must regard whisky as his greatest enemy. The parishioner queried: 'Are we not told in the Bible to love our enemies?' To which the minister cracked back:

Aye, John, aye. But it's no' said that we're to swallow them.

* * *

Sir James Barrie commented:

A young Scotsman of your ability, let loose upon the world, what could he not do? It's almost appalling to think of, especially if he went among the English.

* * *

The chieftain of the Clan MacNab emigrated to Canada with a hundred followers, and, on reaching Toronto, called on his namesake Sir Allan MacNab. He left his card, which bore the words:

The MacNab

Sir Allan next day returned the visit, and left his card. It said, simply:

The Other MacNab

* * *

Dr Rankine, of Glasgow, wrote a rather dull and heavy 'History of France'. Keen to know how it had been taken by the reading public, the author went to Stirling's Library in the city and asked:

'AYE, THE WORLD'S IN A SHOCKIN'
STATE, AN' THE TROUBLE IS THERE'S
NAEWHERE ELSE TAE GO!'

Is Dr Rankine's "History of France" in?' The librarian, Mr Peat, replied:

In! It was never out.

*   *   *

Sandy MacGregor, of Aberdeen, was sent by his lodge to an international convention in New York. When he arrived back in Aberdeen, a friend asked him what he thought of the American people. Sandy said they had not enough sense to go to sleep at night.

'What do you mean?' asked his friend.

'Weel, it's like this,' replied Sandy. 'They kept pounding on my hotel room door at two or three o'clock in the morning.'

'Well, then,' his friend said, 'did you no' answer to see what it was all about?'

Sandy retorted: 'Naw, naw! I just kept playin' my bagpipes.'

*   *   *

A minister with a nice sense of humour, from the Scottish Borders, used to give this address to the bride and bridegroom at wedding ceremonies in his church:

My friends, marriage is a blessing to a few, a curse to many, and a great uncertainty to all.

Do ye venture?

*   *   *

Daft laddies, or village idiots, often win a nod for smart replies. One such was Jamie Fraser, from the parish of Lunan, in Forfarshire. Dean Ramsay tells, in 'Reminiscences of Scottish Life and Character', how the congregation of Jamie's parish had for a time distressed the minister by their habit of sleeping in church. One Sunday Jamie was sitting in the front gallery, wide awake, and many were slumbering around him. The minister tried to waken up the nodding by saying: 'You see, even Jamie Fraser, the idiot, doesn't fall asleep, as so many of you are doing.' Whereupon Jamie, not liking to be so designated, stood up in his pew and said:

Aye, but if I hadnae been an idiot, I micht hae been sleepin', too.

* * *

A young maidservant had been working with a London family for some months before her mistress discovered that she came from Aberdeen. 'But, Mary,' she said, 'why didn't you mention this before?' Said the girl from the North:

Weel, ma'm, it's like this. A didnae like tae boast.

* * *

Two irreverent young men approached their minister in the High Street of Dumfries, and decided to try to confuse him.

'Maister Dunlop,' they said, 'did ye hear the news?'
  'What news?'
  'Oh, the Devil's deid!'

To which the minister, Rev Walter Dunlop, replied: 'Is he? Then I must pray for two fatherless bairns.'

*   *   *

An old farmer in Galloway used to go to church regularly, mainly for the sake of the conversation and gossip among the congregation after the service. On being taken to task for absenting himself, he replied:

Och, there's nae need tae gang tae the kirk noo. Everybody gets a newspaper.

*   *   *

A city officer in Edinburgh had to bury his mother. He hired a hearse, and took her to the family burial place in the Highlands. When he returned with the hearse full of smuggled whisky, he was ribbed about it by a friend. To which he retorted:

Och, man, there's nae harm done. I only took awa' the body and brocht back the speerit!

*   *   *

A girl living in a little village in Aberdeenshire applied for a job at a nearby farm. 'First, you must get me a reference from your previous employer,' said the farmer. Two weeks later the farmer met the girl in Aberdeen and asked if she had been able to get him her 'character'. Replied the girl:

Aye, that A hiv. But A've got yours as weel, an' A'm no' comin'.

*   *   *

A traveller in the Scottish Highlands came on a couple arguing in the road, and asked the reason for the dispute. The man replied:

We're no' deesputin' at a'. We're baith o' the same mind. Ye see, I have a half-croon in my pooch, an' she thinks she's no gaun tae get it – an' I think the same.

*   *   *

A young reporter from Glasgow was flown out by his newspaper to cover the after-effects of a particularly violent earthquake in south-east Europe. He filed a graphic story which opened: 'God sat on a mountain-top here today, and looked down on a scene of . . .' The reporter got a cable back by return from his editor in Glasgow. It said:

Forget earthquake, man! Interview God.

*   *   *

A country laird was promoted to the position of a county magistrate. Meeting his minister, Rev Mr Thom, one day on horseback, the laird joked that he, the minister, was surely more ambitious than his Master who was content to ride on an ass. The Rev Thom replied:

But they canna be gotten noo. They're a' made Justices o' the Peace.

*   *   *

The old country minister was determined to show his congregation the error of their ways, and noticed some young members smiling. Upon which he turned on them and thundered:

Aye, aye, ye may lauch the noo. But when ye're burnin' in that Nethermost Pit, ye'll look up and cry oot, 'Oh Loard, we didna ken, we didna ken.' And the Loard, in His infinite mercy, will look doon on ye an' say, 'Weel, ye ken noo!'

*　　　*　　　*

A minister, praying for Members of Parliament that they might be endowed with wisdom from on high, added the remark:

Aye, Lord, an' ye ken weel they ha'e need o' t.

*　　　*　　　*

Sir Walter Scott was told by his attendant Tom Purdie: 'Them are fine novels o' yours, Sir Walter. They're just invaluable to me.' Sir Walter replied: 'I'm right glad to hear it, Tom.' Upon which Purdie exclaimed:

Aye, indeed, an' when I have been oot a' day hard at wark and come hame tired, I put on the chimley a pint o' porter, an' tak' up ane o' yere novels, and wad ye believe it, sir, I'm asleep directly!

And A' That

The Scotsman usually praises his native land, particularly when far from home. Auld Sandy, from Glasgow, went on a world tour. Enjoying himself in the gaiety of Rome, he told everyone he met: 'Aye, aye. This is a wonderful romantic city, but gie me Glasgow ony time!' In New York, looking up at the skyscrapers, he repeated: 'Aye, aye, wonderful! But you should see the Clyde on a summer's nicht.' It was the same wherever he went – Paris, London, Montreal, Rio. He loved Glasgow better than any of them. On the day he came home, he took a walk through George Square, in the centre of Glasgow, looked around him for five minutes, and was heard to remark:

Och, man, Sandy, whit a bluidy lee!

*   *   *

A Scot, paying a visit to Edinburgh, came away with this description:

Scotland, and particularly Edinburgh, is full of Scots who prefer cognac to whisky, sneer at the kilt, speak with silky Oxford accents, and spend money with the prodigality of Arabian oil sheiks.

*   *   *

Sir Walter Scott, a man not given to easy pronouncements of wit, once commented:

Meat eaten without either mirth or music is ill of digestion.

*   *   *

Robert Burns waxed wittily in this description of Willie Wastle's wife:

> She has an e'e – she has but ane,
>   The cat has twa the very colour;
> Five rusty teeth, furbye a stump.
>   A clapper-tongue wad deave a miller;
> A whiskin' beard about her mou',
>   Her nose and chin they threaten ither –
> Sic a wife as Willie has,
>   I wadna gie a button for her.

*   *   *

Mrs Mary McInroy, of Perth, in the Scottish Highlands, chose a name for her son's home in Perth, Australia:

I chose 'Emahroo'. It spells 'Oor Hame' backwards.

*   *   *

Donald Gibson, in the 'Scottish Daily Record', discussed the claim that, under an old dual-nationality treaty, President de Gaulle of France might well be a Scot, and quipped:

The redoubtable Charles is so pleased with this discovery that he is going to stop saying 'Non'. In future he will say 'Naw'.

*   *   *

A restaurant manager in Edinburgh with a sense of humour put this notice in his window:

SCOTCH HAGGIS with CHIPS!

These tim'rous wee beasties are freshly shot daily in the Highlands for visitors (with ye olde bows and arrows). Skinned alive, heads and legs removed before cooking.

A dish fit for a king. We deport them to all parts of the world!

*   *   *

Sign on a house in the Scottish Highlands:

Costa Plenti.

*   *   *

Clifford Hanley, Scots writer and public wit, has a penetrating eye on the very public business of romance:

The really significant thing about the wooing business today is very simple: everybody's in favour of it. For the first time we have evolved an adult generation which

F

has chucked in the sponge and abandoned the Young Things to their tearaway romances.

Now, when Dad finds a strange young man climbing in at his daughter's window, he borrows half a quid from the intruder, apologises, and promises to stay late at the Bingo session.

* * *

This sign was seen on the wall of a park at Newbattle House, near Edinburgh:

Any person entering this enclosure will be shot <u>and</u> prosecuted.

* * *

Advertisement in the 'Dundee Advertiser':

We congratulate our shareholders on the low rate of *morality* during the past year.

* * *

The Scots couple were courting, and came to a quiet stretch of their walk. Said Donald: 'Jenny, would you object if I should put my arm around your waist?' To which she replied:

Yes, indeed, Donald. I should object, but I might yield to pressure.

* * *

In the Scottish Highlands the long-time dominance of one shipping company has given birth to this witticism in verse:

> The earth belongs unto the Lord
> And all that it contains,
> Except the steamers of the isles
> For they are all MacBrayne's.

*　　　*　　　*

Wise observation from an old Scot:

A salmon from the pool, a wand from the wood, and a deer from the hills are thefts that no man was ever ashamed to own.

*　　　*　　　*

A Presbyterian minister in the reign of King William the Third was preaching in public worship in the Tron Church at Edinburgh. He came to his prayer and observed:

Lord, have mercy upon all fools and idiots, and particularly upon the toon coonsil o' Edinburgh.

*　　　*　　　*

The following lines were found last century, inscribed on the wall of a hostelry near Melrose, in the Scottish Borders:

> This is a good world to live in,
> To lend, to spend, and to give in;

But to get, or to borrow, or keep what's one's own,
'Tis the very worst world that ever was known.

* * *

A modern-day Scottish wit comments:

The old Scots custom of celebrating Hallowe'en isn't what it used to be. Any youngster today knows you can't achieve orbital velocity on a broomstick.

* * *

The farmer's wife went to a chemist's shop in town with two prescriptions, one for her husband, the other for her cow. She found she hadn't enough money to pay for both, and the chemist asked her which she would take. She replied:

Juist give me the stuff for the coo. The morn will do weel eneuch for him, puir man. If he were to dee, I could sune get anither man, but I'm no' sure that I could sae sune get anither coo.

* * *

An old Scots minister, stressing to his congregation the wisdom of repentance, remarked: 'Yes, my friends, unless ye repent, ye shall all perish, just as surely as I'm gaun tae ding the guts oot o' that muckle blue flea that's lichtit on my Bible.' As he was about to strike, the fly got away, whereupon the Scot struck the book with all his strength and exclaimed:

My frien's, there's a chance fur ye yet!

*　　　*　　　*

Sir Walter Scott:

It requires no small talents to be a decided bore.

*　　　*　　　*

Andrew Lang, the Scottish author and editor:

He uses statistics as a drunken man uses lamp-posts – for support rather than for illumination.

*　　　*　　　*

An anonymous Scotsman:

I love my country. I love every inch of it, but if there were no people in it, I'd love it even more.

*　　　*　　　*

An old Scotswoman was told by her friend: 'Hoots, Janet, ye'd think there wis naebody good enough for heaven but yersel' and the meenister!' To which Janet replied:

Deed aye. And sometimes A hae verra grave doots aboot the meenister.

*　　　*　　　*

The wind that blows so fiercely at the top of the famous Waverley Steps in Edinburgh has given rise to this description of an Edinburgh man:

He can be recognised by one particular mannerism – whenever he turns a corner, he puts his hand up to his hat.

*　　*　　*

Sign in a Scottish market-place in the days of stage-coach travel:

God willing, the Duchess of Gordon will leave the Duke's Arms punctually each morning at nine o'clock, except the Sabbath.

*　　*　　*

Robert Burns, on the subject of boasting:

> What of lords with whom you have supped,
>   And of dukes that you dined with yestreen!
> A louse, sir, is still but a louse,
>   Though it crawl on the locks of a queen.

*　　*　　*

An elderly couple chose a Scottish version of the phrase 'Our Own' for their little cottage in the Borders:

Wirrain

*　　*　　*

An old Gaelic witticism:

> Everyone can rule a shrew
> Except the one he's married to.

*   *   *

The wit of this saying, too often heard in Scotland in the past, is not to be commended, and is quoted with reservations:

Ach, he's nae guid. A kent his faither.

(A real case of 'A prophet being without honour in his own country'.)

*   *   *

A writer in a Scottish daily newspaper:

Any girl can be glamorous. All you have to do is to stand still and look stupid.

*   *   *

The minister of a wee church in the Scottish Highlands was preaching a strong sermon about the evils of drink, and kept telling the congregation not to imbibe too frequently. He concluded:

We'll no' mak' this sermon owre personal, but if a short, bald-headed laird sittin' in the corner o' the east gallery pew tak's it to himsel', I canna help it.

*   *   *

An old Scotsman married a young wife, thirty years his junior. When his friends queried him on the disparity of their ages, he told them: 'She will be near me to close my een' (eyes). Whereupon the witty one among his friends remarked:

A weel, I've had twa wives, and they *opened* mine!

*   *   *

A Pole whose name was quite unpronounceable by any average Britisher was keen to play a game of golf at St Andrews. He approached the starter three times and asked that he be put down to play the next morning at ten. On his fourth attempt he was confronted by a determined Scot who looked him straight in the face and said:

Ye'll come the day after tomorrow at eleven o'clock, and ye'll answer tae the name o' Macpherson.

*   *   *

A reporter visited an eighty-five-year-old Scotsman to interview him on his formula for a long life. 'Weel, it's guid livin',' the old man explained. 'A never drink or stay oot late at nicht.' Just then there was an awful commotion downstairs, and the reporter asked what all the noise was about. To which the old Scotsman replied:

Och, that's juist ma faither! He's been oot on a bender again!

*   *   *

A Scotsman gave this description of the kind of church minister he most admired:

Nane o' your guid-warks men, or preachers o' cauld morality for me! Gie me a speerit-rousin' preacher that'll haud the deil under the noses o' the congregation and mak' their flesh creep.

*   *   *

A Scotswoman in the Highlands quoted to her husband the old Gaelic proverb 'Foadaidh cat sealltainn air an righ', meaning 'The Cat may look at the King'. To which the husband quickly replied:

True, but the King may put the eyes out of the Cat.

*   *   *

A Scottish newspaper comment:

A woman is never loved for her virtues, so what's the good of having any?

*   *   *

A correspondent in another Scottish newspaper:

He was the kind of man whose wife had a keen sense of rumour.

*   *   *

A modern young miss in Edinburgh:

What I find wonderful is how my mother learned all the things she keeps telling me to shun.

*   *   *

A town-crier who worked for the Duke of Argyll announced to the neighbouring community:

Ta hoy! Ta hoy! By command of Her Majesty, King George, an' her Grace the Duke o' Argyll. If anybody is found fishin' aboon the loch, below the loch, afore the loch, or ahint the loch, in the loch or on the loch, aroon the loch, or aboot the loch, she's to be persecutit wiss three terrible persecutions; first, she's to be burnt, syne she's to be drownt, an' then she's to be hangt – an' if ever she comes back she's to be persecutit wiss a far waur death. God save the King and Her Grace the Duke of Argyll.

*   *   *

Proclamation from the pulpit of Luss Church, on Loch Lomond-side:

O yiss! O yiss! O yiss! There will be no Lord's Day here next Sabbath, because the Laird's wife will have a muckle washin', and she needs the kirk to dry her claes in.

*   *   *

A Scots father, keen to correct the manners of his impatient and hungry son, worded his grace:

For what we are about to receive, and for what Tam has already received, do Thou O Lord make us truly thankful.

*   *   *

The old lady asked her nephew, a not-too-successful minister, why he had entered the Church. He replied: 'Because I was called.' To which she quietly retorted:

James, are you sure it wasn't some other noise you heard?

*   *   *

Some Scots humour is heavy-handed. Bill Tennent, a television commentator, was out walking the day after one of his TV shows when a workman high on a roof gave him a friendly 'hi-ya' sign, then beckoned him towards him. Bill crossed the street, dodged the traffic, stood below the building with a smile on his face, and waited for the expected approbation. The workman leaned over from the top of the roof and, in a knowing voice, called out:

Hi, Bill. See yon programme o' yours last night. See yon. it was —— lousy!

*   *   *

The Reverend John Robertson, of Stirling, a stern opponent of smoking, declared from his pulpit (note 'reek' = smoke):

If God had meant man to smoke, then surely He wad ha'e made a hole in the croon o' his heid to let oot the reek.

* * *

'JIST WHEN AH WIS DAEIN' THE TON MA 'L' PLATES BLEW AFF!'

A Glasgow town councillor, on being promoted to a Bailie, gave a fine banquet at which his health was drunk. Replying, he said:

I canna say I'm no' kind o' entitled to this honour, for, believe me, I've gone through a' the various stages o' degradation to reach it.

* * *

Jamie's wife left him and went to live with her mother. A friend consoled him and said what an awful pity she had departed. The man replied: 'Oh, but she could do worse yet.' 'What worse can she do than that?' queried the friend. To which Jamie said, sorrowfully:

She can come back again!

* * *

An old Scottish Highlander, commending moderation in all things, commented:

Man, I've made twa rules a' ma life, an' I've kept tae them.
    First, never tae drink whisky without water.
    Second, never tae drink water without whisky.

* * *

Sir James M Barrie (note 'critters' = creatures):

Has it ever struck you that the trouts bite best on the Sabbath? God's critters tempting decent men.

In Their Cups

Whisky – Scotch whisky – is the native drink of Scotland, and huge supplies of it go all round the world. So it's natural that many observations are concerned with the social habit of 'enjoyin' a wee dram':

The old Scotsman was asked by a friend what he thought of his nearest neighbour. He replied:

Och, weel, he's a decent-like lad, but he's no' exactly a temperance man. He was sittin' there juist drinkin' an' drinkin', until I could scarcely see him.

*   *   *

The lady of the farm-house was not renowned for her generosity in pouring drinks. She handed her shepherd a drink and remarked that it was extra-special, being fourteen years old. The old shepherd raised his glass solemnly and said:

Weel, ma lady, there's one thing for sure. It's verra small for its age.

*   *   *

A tyrannical wife in Inverness tried to stop her husband from drinking by employing her brother to act the part of a ghost, and so frighten him on the way home from a drinking session. As the apparition appeared before him, the husband asked: 'And wha are you?' 'I am Auld Nick,' was the reply. To which the husband, still very much in his cups, retorted:

Man, are ye really? Come awa', noo, and gi'e's a shake o' your hand. I'm mairret to a sister o' yours.

*　　*　　*

A country laird was being driven home by his manservant after a merry evening with a fellow-laird in the Highlands. He had been given a cherry brandy in error for port, and was in a capricious and dignified mood. They hit a lonely part of the moors, and the laird's hat and wig blew off. The servant ran to retrieve them. He handed his master the hat, and the latter took it but declined the wig, saying: 'It's no' my wig, lad. It's no' my wig.' The manservant, impatient, quipped:

Ye'd better tak' it, sir. There's no muckle choice o' wigs on Munrimmon Muir.

*　　*　　*

When a tradesman finishes a job at a house in Scotland, it is a good old custom to offer him a wee drink.

'Would you like a wee dram?' the lady-of-the-house asked a joiner.

'A wouldna' say No,' he replied.

The lady produced the bottle. 'How do you like it, Sandy?' she asked.

He replied: Half whisky and half water. An' pit in plenty o' water.

*   *   *

The two old Scots had imbibed overmuch. Saying his good-night, the one told the other:

John, man, when ye gang oot at the door, ye'll see twa cabs. Tak' the first yin – the t'ither ane's no' there!

Wit and Wisdom

Proverbs have been described as little nutshell phrases or sentences incorporating the wit of one and the wisdom of many. Scots proverbs do not bely that description, as these examples show:

Let that flea stick tae the wa'.
  (Say no more on the subject)

*   *   *

You're nae chicken for a' your cheepin'.
  (Despite the noise you make, you're no youngster)

*   *   *

Mony cooks ne'er made gude kail.
  (Too many cooks spoil the broth)

*   *   *

A gangin' fit is aye gettin'.
  (A man of industry will always get a living)

*   *   *

Ye canna tak' the breeks aff a Heilan'man, for he has nane on!
(note 'breeks'=trousers)

* * *

Sir Walter Scott, in 'The Heart of Midlothian', gives this useful advice:

Jock, when ye hae naething else to do, yet ye may aye be sticking in a tree; it will be growing, Jock, when ye're sleeping.

* * *

Ae bird i' the hand is worth twa fleein'.
  (A bird in the hand is worth two in the bush)

* * *

Mony sma's mak' a muckle.
  (Many little things result in riches)

* * *

There's nocht sae queer as fowk.

* * *

Ye're feared for a day ye never saw.

* * *

Dinna shape shune by your ain shauchlie feet!

*   *   *

This old proverb, like so many of its kind, epitomises the wit of the Scot over the generations:

> They say, in Fife,
> That – next to nae wife –
> The best thing is a guid wife.

*   *   *

Still another poses the interesting question:

A' are guid lasses, but where do a' the ill wives come frae?

*   *   *

Ilka cock craws best on his ain middenheid.

*   *   *

A fule an' his siller's sune parted.

*   *   *

He's like a hen on a hot girdle.

*   *   *

LOOK! PHOEBE - TAKIN'
THE DEVALUED POUND
INTAE CONSIDERATION —
AHVE LOST WEIGHT.

Hold your hands aff ither folks' bairns till ye get some of your ain.

* * *

The loudest bummer's no' the best bee.

* * *

The De'il's aye guid tae his ain.

* * *

Mony a mickle mak's a muckle.

* * *

A fu' purse ne'er lacks friends.

* * *

Gie him rope eneuch, an' he'll hang himsel'.

* * *

Ye canna mak' a silk purse o' a soo's lug

(note 'lug'=ear)

* * *

An ounce o' mither's wit is worth a pound o' clergy.

* * *

Scots used to voice this excuse when someone in a house broke wind:

Better a toom (empty) hoose than an ill tenant.

* * *

Silence and thocht hurt nae man.

* * *

Robert Louis Stevenson, on the state of marriage:

If we take matrimony at its lowest, we regard it as a sort of friendship recognised by the police.

* * *

On a link common to every man, woman and child:

Everyone lives by selling something.

* * *

A nod's as guid as a wink to a blin' horse.

* * *

Robert Burns gave the world a pithy gem of wit and wisdom in 'To A Mouse':

The best-laid schemes o' mice and men gang aft agley.

* * *

More wit – and with a moral, too – from Robert Louis Stevenson in these lines:

> The world is so full of a number of things,
> I'm sure we should all be as happy as kings.

* * *

Beggars shouldna be choosers.

* * *

Ne'er marry a widow unless her first man wis hanged.

* * *

The proof o' the puddin' is in the eatin' o't.

* * *

Fools and bairns shouldna see half-done work.

* * *

Better sma' fish than nane.

*   *   *

He that gets gear, before he gets wit,
Is but a short time the master o' it.

*   *   *

Hang a thief when he's young, an' he'll no' steal when he's auld.

*   *   *

Be aye the thing ye would be ca'd.

*   *   *

It's no' lost what a frien' gets.

*   *   *

When gossipin' wives meet, the De'il gangs tae his dinner.

*   *   *

There's aye some water whaur the stirkie droons.

*   *   *

Robert Louis Stevenson said:

To travel hopefully is a better thing than to arrive.

* * *

Sir Walter Scott:

> Oh, what a tangled web we weave,
> When first we practise to deceive.

* * *

An old Highland proverb:

> Here's tae ye a' yer days,
> Plenty meat an' plenty claes;
> Plenty parritch, and a horn spune,
> And anither tattie when a's dune.

* * *

Another Scots proverb:

A sillerless man gaes fast through the market.

* * *

An old Gaelic proverb:

The Irishman's wit is on the tip of his tongue; the Gael is wise after the event.

*   *   *

Another Gaelic proverb:

One can protect himself from a thief, but not from a liar.

*   *   *

Thomas Carlyle:

The greatest of faults, I should say, is to be conscious of none.

*   *   *

Andrew Carnegie:

The man who dies rich dies disgraced.

*   *   *

An old proverb:

What maun be, maun be.

*   *   *

Sir Walter Scott, in 'The Heart of Midlothian':

The De'il's no' sae ill as he's ca'd.

*   *   *

A blate (timid) cat mak's a prood moose.

*   *   *

Dinna gut your fish till ye get them.

*   *   *

Far awa' fowls hae fine feathers.

*   *   *

God send ye mair sense, an' me mair siller.

*   *   *

Thomas Carlyle:

He that hath a secret should not only hide it, but hide that
he has it to hide.

*   *   *

Gems of wit and wisdom from the old Gaelic tongue:

The fool may pass for wise if he holds his tongue.

Say but little and say it well.

It is no secret when three know it.

If you cannot bite, do not show your teeth.

The slow horse will reach the mill,
   But the one that breaks its bones will not.

*   *   *

A Scots wit in the nineteenth century commented:

The dividing line between bad and good is being found out.

*   *   *

More proverbs from the Gaelic:

Choose your wife with her night-cap on.

There is meat and music here, as the fox said when he ran
away with the bagpipes.

The oar that's nearest at hand, row with it.

Despise your old shoes when you get your new ones.

There never was good or ill without a woman being concerned in it.

Marriage will sober love.

Going to ruin is silent work.

The heaviest ear of corn bends its head the lowest.

Stray dogs and other people's children.

* * *

Lord Dewar:

He is a wise man who noes a lot.

* * *

John Buchan:

We can pay our debt to the past by putting the future in debt to ourselves.

* * *

Thomas Carlyle:

Genius means a transcendent capacity for taking trouble, first of all.

* * *

Sir James Barrie, in an address at Edinburgh University:

As Dr Johnson never said, is there a Scotsman without charm?

*   *   *

Robert Louis Stevenson:

A friend is a present you give yourself.

There is so much good in the worst of us, and so much bad in the best of us, that it behoves all of us not to talk about the rest of us.

*   *   *

Two final proverbs from the Gaelic:

What's guid tae gie shouldna' be ill tae tak'.

Three can keep a secret if twa be awa'.

Acknowledgements

The wit and humour of the Scots over the centuries is extensive, and due thanks must be given to many sources, too numerous to be listed in full. In most instances the credit is given with the witticism in the relevant chapter, and the originator of the comment is mentioned. To these, from the past and the present, acknowledgement is given.

For the various cartoons I gratefully acknowledge the ready co-operation of Ewen Bain, Bud Neill, William Gall, and Jimmy Malcolm, and of the editors of the *Evening Times*, *Evening Citizen*, and the *Scottish Daily Express*.